JOURNEY
—TO THE—
SELF

An Interactive Workbook and Journal with 52 Life Lessons Based on Yoga Philosophy

Sandi Greenberg, RYT-500

October 2015
Dear Katie, your
May be filled
journey Wonder and
with beauty.
Love, Sandi

Journey to the Self

Copyright © 2012 by Sandi Greenberg. All Rights Reserved.

For information about this title or to order other books and/or electronic media, contact the publisher:
Tandu Publications
428 E. Thunderbird Road, #123
Phoenix, Arizona 85022
www.NoPlaceLikeOmYoga.com
NoPlaceLikeOm@hotmail.com

Library of Congress Control Number: 2012947983

ISBN: 978-0-9841918-4-0

Printed in the United States of America

Cover and Interior design: 1106 Design

DEDICATION

In memory of my brother, David Allen Chez,
whose spirit continues to guide me on my path

INTRODUCTION

"And you? When will you begin your long journey into yourself?"
~JALAL AD-DIN RUMI

THIS BOOK HAS RESULTED FROM my desire to share with as many people as possible the gifts of Eastern (yoga) philosophy and practice that have benefited me to such a great extent in my life. My first book, *Your Yoga Experience,* is a practical guide to a physical as well as spiritual practice. *Journey to the Self,* however, focuses on the mental and spiritual realms. Not only does the book offer another 52 philosophies and suitable quotations to encourage self-inquiry, but additional reflection is encouraged through journaling prompts and journal pages on which to write one's thoughts.

THE LOTUS FLOWER, seen on the cover of this book, is an important Hindu symbol of spiritual growth, awakening, and transformation. This flower grows out of the mud (our ignorance) and blossoms above the water into the light of day (enlightenment). As it aspires toward the light, its petals open into a beautiful flower, as we do during our personal growth on our journey toward knowing our true Self.

SELF-REFLECTION, or *svadyaya* in Sanskrit, is an important and challenging part of any journey, especially a mental/emotional/spiritual journey to the Self. Learning to truly know oneself takes a lifetime, to be sure, but I propose that one's truth, happiness, goal attainment, and personal satisfaction cannot fully be reached at any stage without the pursuit of *svadyaya,* to whatever extent. The philosophies and concepts presented in this book can only be studied and understood in terms of your own attitudes, beliefs, and inner sense of knowing. If you indulge in introspection and reflection, then journal freely, you will learn about yourself. Your conscious and subconscious thoughts and personal truths will arise if you let them flow from the mind through your fingers and onto the page.

FROM MY EXPERIENCE as a school teacher, mentor, yoga instructor, life coach and hypnotherapist, it seems that the greatest epiphanies which have lead to progress when feeling stuck in life have come from the kind of introspection that is encouraged in *Journey to the Self.* After reading a stimulating idea or quote, we don't always apply it to ourselves. We often block or are in denial about our truth, our intentions, our motivations, and our habits. When allowing your thoughts to flow spontaneously in response to a prompt, you can uncover the source of a problem, the beginning of a solution, or a glint of who you are. You may be amazed at yourself and fascinated by the truths that arise within you!

THERE ARE MANY WAYS TO JOURNAL. Like so many other endeavors, journaling styles depend upon one's individual personality, habits and perspective. In *Journey to the Self,* each reflection or lesson offers you a *topic or theme* presented through the lens of some philosophy, and then poses questions to trigger your thoughts and insights. If you wish to journal further on a topic, I offer other techniques below with the invitation to try them and choose whichever style brings you the most satisfaction, spontaneity, and peace of mind.

In *stream of consciousness* journaling, start writing as though you are talking to someone, without worrying about form, punctuation or spelling. Let it all just pour out of you so that you don't have to think about it again during your day. When you're finished, you can either let it remain as written without rereading it, or go back and reread it, highlighting things you may want to respond to or comment on in your journaling at another time. It's surprising what may come to the surface when you allow your subconscious free reign.

Another journaling suggestion is *letter writing*. After journaling about an idea from one of the themes in the book or on one of your own topics, write a hypothetical letter to someone. Get what is bothering you off your chest without actually mailing it. Once you have let go of the emotion that needs to come out, the letter can be destroyed or reread if the old bothersome thoughts reappear. In addition, you may be moved to write about new experiences or perspectives that result from your journaling.

Literary note taking is helpful when reading this book or any other book. As you read, take notes for future personal journaling. Write down your favorite quotes and the page numbers on which they appear. Write your response to—or thoughts about—the quote or the memory that it triggered. You can also record any questions that may arise for future journaling ideas or discussions with others. Enjoy yourself while releasing and bringing to awareness pent up emotions, resentments, or both, all the while getting closer to knowing your true Self.

THE INTENTIONS in this book are there to help you focus on a positive idea or goal you want to reinforce for yourself throughout your day. How you begin your day often sets the tone for the remainder of the day. In *Journey to the Self,* each reflection or lesson includes a suggestion for an intention plus the space to write your own if you prefer. The idea is to create a vision of the life you want or the way you want to be. By stating your intention and repeating it throughout your day, you put your intention out into the world and remind yourself of your vision. I like Phillip Moffitt's definition of intention as "...essentially the capacity to stay in touch with the core values that you wish to live by as you pursue your life's goals and engage with others. Being grounded in your intention literally changes what you perceive in a situation and how your mind interprets what you perceive; it also affects how you act on what you perceive."

JOURNEY TO THE SELF is an interactive workbook to be read and written in for enjoyment, introspection, and personal growth. It is for your own personal curiosity or to be read and discussed with others. Either way, you are invited to observe the transformation that will quite naturally result from your new self-awareness and self-knowledge as you begin your life's amazing journey to your Self. While there is a beginning, there is no end in sight to the wonders you will uncover.

JOURNEY TO THE SELF
Sandi Greenberg

Writing, thinking, introspection
Namaste or genuflection
Torah, sutras, meditation—
It's all a journey to the Self.

Kindness, truth, and non-attachment
Purity, surrender, unconditional contentment
Concentration, discipline, other holy sentiment—
Guides us in the journey to the Self.

That same Self that's with us all our days on Earth
The same one we've struggled with since our time of birth
How long must it take us till we know our worth—
It's all part of the journey to the Self.

A bit of philosophy to give the day a start
A daily intention to engage the universe's part
Sitting down to journal and unburden the heart—
Helps along the journey to the Self.

It begins with consciousness, awareness, and breath
Continues through openness, reflection, and depth
If lucky an epiphany before what we call 'death'—
All thanks to the journey to the Self.

And if we don't learn our lessons before our time is through
It's said it all begins again, it all evolves anew
So open up your mind and heart and trust in what is true—
Enjoy your ride on your journey to the Self.

Table of Contents

I
LIVING AND LOVING
THE JOURNEY

WE ALL EXPERIENCE DISAPPOINTMENTS and bumpy patches throughout our lives and we would be wise to learn the difficult lesson of patience to help us get through these rough patches. By taking to heart the idea that there is a purpose for everything, you can look at your present experience and, with introspection, try to understand what can be learned and perhaps even why you have to go through it before progressing onward. Finding some value in each step of the journey may make it easier to wait for the sought-after destination or result. One of the many beautiful rewards of surrendering to living in the present is the enjoyment of what is happening only at this moment, then the next, then the next, which eliminates the pain of the past and the "what ifs" of the future.

"The wind was against them now, and Piglet's ears streamed behind him like banners as he fought his way along, and it seemed hours before he got them into the shelter of the Hundred Acre Wood and they stood up straight again, to listen, a little nervously to the roaring of the gale among the tree tops.

'Supposing a tree fell down, Pooh, when we were underneath it?'
'Supposing it didn't,' said Pooh after careful thought."

~A.A. MILNE

INTENTION: "I am just where I am supposed to be."

or

Write your own: _____

_____

"I haven't a clue as to how my story will end. But that's all right. When you set out on a journey and night covers the road, you don't conclude the road has vanished. And how else could we discover the stars?"

~AUTHOR UNKNOWN

REFLECTIONS: As you experience any disappointments or rough patches during the course of your day, "how" and "why" questions may arise from these experiences. Be aware of the answers that may come to you and what you may be able to learn from them. If answers don't come, try to get to a place where you can just appreciate and learn from the questions and whatever might present itself. Breathe and concentrate on the moment, rather than allow an indulgence in the past or an anticipation of the "What Ifs" of the future. Now reflect on what you perceive your obstacles may be to achieving your goals. What are you prepared to do to overcome them while you wait patiently?

Journey to the Self

2
FEELING ALIVE

THERE ARE INDIVIDUALS WHO HAVE so protected themselves from pain, from possible negative consequences, or from challenges that threaten failure, that they inadvertently "protect" themselves from pleasure, positive experiences and successes as well. When facing an uncomfortable challenge that you objectively feel would benefit you, ask yourself: "What is the worst thing that can happen? Can I handle that?" If the answer is "yes," then jump in with both feet, take a chance and feel alive!

"Said a sheet of snow-white paper, 'Pure was I created, and pure will I remain forever. I would rather be burnt and turn to white ashes than suffer darkness to touch me or the unclean to come near me.'

The ink bottle heard what the paper was saying, and it laughed in its dark heart; but it never dared to approach her. And the multi-colored pencils heard her also, and they too never came near her.

And the snow-white sheet of paper did remain pure and chaste for ever—pure and chaste—and empty."

~KAHLIL GIBRAN

INTENTION: "I am ready to take chances and feel alive."

or

Write your own: _____

_____

"Twenty years from now you will be more disappointed by the things you didn't do than by the things you did. So throw off the bowlines, sail away from the safe harbor, catch the trade winds in your sails. Explore. Dream. Discover."

~MARK TWAIN

REFLECTIONS: What challenges have caused you to feel anxiety? What might be the cause of your feelings? What things have you wanted to do but shielded yourself from doing? What good things might happen if you let your protective shield down?

_____

_____

_____

_____

_____

_____

_____

_____

_____

_____

_____

_____

_____

_____

_____

_____

_____

Journey to the Self

3
PERSPECTIVE

Y our individual perspective on any given situation is subjective, or personal, meaning that each person has a different perspective on the same thing. This difference in perspective can readily be observed when speaking with friends after an event. Even though the event was attended by all, the descriptions your friends give of the event and their feelings about it are so different from your own that you wonder if you all shared the same experience! Likewise, if you could attend the same event more than once—each time in a different mood—your experience of it may be totally different from time to time. We tend to project our inner reality onto the outer reality. Which is real? The more objective and realistic you can be in a given situation, the more you can connect with your true intentions and feelings and get to know who you really are. In addition, you can better respond to the situation when your perspective is coming from a centered, balanced place rather than reacting only from an emotional point of view.

"If we have a positive mental attitude, then even when surrounded by hostility, we shall not lack inner peace. On the other hand, if our mental attitude is more negative, influenced by fear, suspicion, helplessness, or self-loathing, then even when surrounded by our best friends, in a nice atmosphere and comfortable surroundings, we shall not be happy."

~THE DALAI LAMA

INTENTION: "I stand back and observe my reality without judgment."

or

Write your own: _____

_____

"There's what's happening and there's our version of what's happening. It's our version that causes us suffering."

~KRISHNA DAS

REFLECTIONS: While participating in the various activities throughout your day, notice how your inner mood and degree of happiness affects your experience of those activities. Then, connecting to breath, try to stand back and observe what is happening as objectively as possible. Is there is a difference in the experiences when you come from an objective perspective?

_____

_____

_____

_____

_____

_____

_____

_____

_____

_____

_____

_____

_____

_____

_____

🪷 Journey to the Self

4
HOW IS THAT
WORKING FOR YOU?

E INSTEIN SAID: "Insanity is doing the same thing over and over
again, but expecting different results." Repeating the same words in
order to change someone's behavior is like speaking louder and louder
to a person who doesn't speak your language or who is totally deaf.
Whether the problem or situation is large or small, if your response
is to keep trying the same old things and then feel frustrated by the
same old outcomes, ask yourself the question: "How is that working
for me?" If the answer is that it's not, perhaps it's time to change your
dynamic and create a new paradigm.

"If you always do what you've always done, you'll always get what you've always gotten."

~TONY ROBBINS

INTENTION: "I am open to new thoughts and ideas."

or

Write your own: _____

_____

"You cannot solve a problem with the same mind that created it."

~ALBERT EINSTEIN

REFLECTIONS: Each time you reflect upon something you've done or a situation you're in, check in with yourself by asking: "How is that working for me?" An honest answer can either change your perspective and challenge you to try something new, or give you reason to pat yourself on the back...until the next time you ask. Journal about what you tend to keep doing and the results of those actions. Now try to come up with different actions that may lead to positive solutions.

_____

_____

_____

_____

_____

_____

_____

_____

_____

_____

_____

_____

_____

_____

_____

_____

_____

_____

_____

_____

_____

_____

_____

_____

_____

_____

_____

_____

_____

_____

_____

_____

_____

_____

Journey to the Self

5
ATTACHMENT
TO RESULTS

WHEN YOU APPROACH AN ACTIVITY, a friendship or a journey with a fixed idea of what it should look like, you often set yourself up for disappointment or failure by not allowing yourself to be open to whatever may arise in the moment outside of that set plan. For example, if you approach your yoga practice or other pastime with a determination to deepen a pose or find relaxation, you may miss out on what actually arises during that time. If you can release your set agenda while exercising patience and compassion toward yourself, you might be pleasantly surprised to see what you do experience in the moment.

"Having no fixed plans, having no agenda, opens us up to listen, to be inquisitive, explore, get lost, be fluid and to go with the the flow. Sometimes when we plan too much…we can become rigid in our expectations, unable to listen to what may arise, and forget about living in the present moment."

~MEL CAMPBELL

INTENTION: "I have no agenda and am open to the moment."

or

Write your own: _____

_____

"Adopt the pace of nature: her secret is patience."

~RALPH WALDO EMERSON

REFLECTIONS: Instead of engaging in your daily activities with a set of expectations, apply patience both to yourself and others, and release your set agenda. Journal about your experience and your reaction.

_____

_____

_____

_____

_____

_____

_____

_____

_____

_____

_____

_____

_____

_____

_____

_____

_____

Journey to the Self

6
FREEDOM

WHAT DOES FREEDOM MEAN TO YOU? The word conjures up many questions for me. Is freedom the right to choose who we want to be and what we want to do without being thwarted? Can we really feel free if we remain enslaved by our own minds, which may limit our sense of what is possible, prevent us from forgiving others, or tie us to our respective pasts? Are we free if we physically or emotionally enslave other sentient beings? Are we motivated by going toward something or running away from something else? We must each answer these questions for ourselves because we each have a different concept of freedom based on our individual life experiences or cultural histories, which will impact our behavior toward ourselves and others.

"I know but one freedom and that is the freedom of the mind."

~ANTOINE DE SAINT-EXUPERY

INTENTION: "I am free to determine my own life."

or

Write your own: _____

_____

*"From this hour I ordain myself loos'd of limits and imaginary
    lines,*
going where I list, my own master total and absolute,
listening to others, considering well what they say,
pausing, searching, receiving, contemplating,
*gently, but with undeniable will divesting myself of the holds
    that would hold me."*

~WALT WHITMAN

REFLECTIONS: Think of your own definition of freedom. Reflect upon and journal about the questions posed in this lesson. How might your answers affect your day-to-day living and decisions?

_____

_____

_____

_____

_____

_____

_____

_____

_____

_____

_____

_____

_____

_____

_____

_____

_____

_____

_____

_____

_____

_____

_____

_____

_____

_____

_____

_____

_____

_____

_____

_____

_____

_____

_____

_____

_____

_____

_____

Journey to the Self

7
DEALING WITH REALITY

STATED SIMPLY, UNHAPPINESS comes from your mind wanting things to be different than they are. You may find yourself
constantly struggling with your mind in your quest to change the
reality of any given situation. However, by dealing with what is in
the moment rather than what "should be," stillness and peace can be
found more easily.

"The primary cause of unhappiness is never the situation, but your thoughts about it. Be aware of the thoughts you are thinking. Separate them from the situation, which is always neutral, which always is as it is. There is a situation or the fact, and here are my thoughts about it. Instead of making up stories, stay with the facts. For example, 'I am ruined' is a story. It limits you and prevents you from taking effective action. 'I have 50 cents left in my bank account' is a fact. Facing facts is always empowering."

~ECKHART TOLLE

INTENTION: "I deal with what is, not with what should be."

or

Write your own: _____

_____

"The mind seems to be profoundly ill at ease with the present moment. Mind cannot seem to rest with 'how it is' right now. I sometimes call this the War With Reality."

~STEPHEN COPE

REFLECTIONS: As you go through your day, notice what causes you frustration or angst and then let go—perhaps standing outside of the situation in the objectivity of Witness Consciousness (objectively witnessing yourself). Journal about how you are served when you take control and don't allow your mind to sabotage you.

_____

_____

_____

_____

_____

_____

_____

_____

_____

_____

_____

_____

_____

_____

_____

Journey to the Self

8

APPRECIATION

THE FOUR STEPS TO HAPPINESS and success according to Og Mandino in his book, *The Greatest Miracle in the World,* are to count your blessings, proclaim your rarity, go another mile, and use wisely your power of choice. How can these steps be applied to your life? Notice the beauty and the wonder around you everywhere; appreciate that you are unique in how you can see, hear, feel, and experience this miraculous Nature; don't settle for the mediocre but go that extra mile to help yourself, your fellow human beings, and all living things including our Earth; and choose to love rather than hate, nurture rather than destroy, and be active in your life rather than passive and a victim.

"There is hope if people will begin to awaken that spiritual part of themselves, that heartfelt knowledge that we are caretakers of this planet."

~BROOKE "MEDICINE EAGLE" EDWARDS

INTENTION: "I choose to be aware of the beauty around me."

or

Write your own: _____

_____

"We need to consider how our actions, in affecting the environment, are likely to affect others. This is often difficult to judge; but it is clear that we are the only species with the power to destroy the earth. Birds and insects have no such power, nor does any other mammal. Yet if we have the capacity to destroy the earth, we also have the capacity to protect it. I believe we have an urgent responsibility to do so."

~THE DALAI LAMA

REFLECTIONS: How can you go that extra mile for yourself, other beings and your planet? What choices will you make that will enhance and honor your rarity and that of others?

_____

_____

_____

_____

_____

_____

_____

_____

_____

_____

_____

_____

_____

_____

_____

_____

_____

_____

_____

_____

_____

_____

_____

_____

_____

_____

_____

_____

_____

_____

_____

_____

_____

_____

_____

_____

9
ALL ABOUT ATTITUDE

IT ALWAYS COMES DOWN TO attitude, doesn't it? You can choose to approach daily events as problems and things to fix, or as interesting occurrences to be looked at with curiosity and perhaps humor. You can then decide to go about living that way. It really depends on how you want to experience your life. The choice is yours.

"So often times it happens,
We all live our life in chains,
And we never even know we have the key."

~THE EAGLES

INTENTION: "My attitude colors my experience."

or

Write your own: _____

_____

"Every day may not be good, but there's something good in
every day."

~AUTHOR UNKNOWN

REFLECTIONS: Journal about the good things that occur during your day. What positive aspects can you find about any events that you originally perceived as negative?

_____

_____

_____

_____

_____

_____

_____

_____

_____

_____

_____

_____

_____

_____

_____

_____

_____

Journey to the Self

10
VALIDATION

How often do you walk down a street or through a store and not notice the people around you, smile at them, or say hello? We all seek validation of our existence, the lack of which may lead to depression in some individuals who are going through a difficult time in life. Likewise, we may not take the time to notice and acknowledge the positive things about ourselves, though we may be quick to judge and criticize. Don't be afraid to give others or yourself a compliment or greeting, which may be the only bright spot or act of caring in a person's day.

"No one is invisible."

NELSON MANDELA

INTENTION: "I acknowledge myself and others around me."

or

Write your own: _____

_____

"Too often we underestimate the power of a touch, a smile, a kind word, a listening ear, an honest compliment, or the smallest act of caring, all of which have the potential to turn a life around."

~LEO BUSCAGLIA

REFLECTIONS: Consciously notice the people around you as you go through your day. Offer a compliment, make a friendly comment, or somehow acknowledge other people. Journal about their reactions as well as how acknowledging people may have positively colored your day.

_____

_____

_____

_____

_____

_____

_____

_____

_____

_____

_____

_____

_____

_____

Journey to the Self

II

ALL THINGS IN
MODERATION

SOMETIMES LIFE THROWS US extreme situations. Other times we create our own situations with our all-or-nothing attitudes and labels of "success" or "failure." Our society seems to promote extremes. For example, some people suffer from anorexia while others adopt dieting fads of every type, leading to over-eating addictions. Some people are habitual couch potatoes, while others exercise obsessively until no body fat remains. There are also those who are workaholics and those who are underachievers. The list is endless. In yoga, the middle ground is sought—that place of equanimity where peace might be found. Balance and moderation can be one road to peace of mind.

"Moderation. Small helpings. Sample a little bit of everything. These are the secrets of happiness and good health."

~JULIA CHILD

INTENTION: "I enjoy balance and moderation in my endeavors."

or

Write your own: _____

_____

"Even a happy life cannot be without a measure of darkness, and the word happy would lose its meaning if it were not balanced by sadness. It is far better to take things as they come along with patience and equanimity."

~CARL GUSTAV JUNG

REFLECTIONS: Which areas of your life do you feel are out of balance? Journal about your habits, then brainstorm how you can introduce a bit more moderation into your life. Record your results and see how moderation serves you instead.

_____

_____

_____

_____

_____

_____

_____

_____

_____

_____

_____

_____

_____

_____

_____

_____

Journey to the Self

12
THE BEST YOU CAN BE

*P*IEDRO WAS A SHOEMAKER *who lived at the edge of the village. He was a craftsman, who took great delight in making each shoe as perfect as it could be. But although he worked long and hard all his life to support his wife and five children, he remained very poor.*

In the evenings, he would go home with the little money he had made during the day, and give it to his wife to buy food. And she would take the money and sigh and say, "You're a good man, Piedro." But she would look at him with sad eyes that bore holes in his soul and he would eat very little so that there would be more food for the children. Then he would sit in the old frayed armchair in the corner of the room and play his mouth-organ and he would let the music wash over him and help him to forget that his wife was sad and his children were hungry.

And so Piedro lived out his days. His children grew up and left home to make their own way in the world. And Piedro made shoes, each one as perfect as it could be, and he played his mouth-organ and his wife watched him, and sometimes she would put a gentle hand on his knee. One evening, he quietly died.

When he arrived at the gates of heaven, Piedro was met by an Archangel. He confided to the Angel that he was very worried about meeting the Creator of all Life. In explanation, he said that he was worried because in his life he had been just a simple shoemaker. He hadn't done all the things that he should have done, nor been all the things he should have been.

"I did not act as nobly as my father, nor as cleverly as my brother; I did not behave as gently as my mother, nor as wisely as the village chief; I did not provide for my wife and children as well as my friends provided for their families, nor was I as rich in good deeds as my beloved wife." The Archangel looked at Piedro and smiled a gentle smile.

"My friend," he said, "There is only one question that the Creator of all Life will ask you."

"What is that?"

"Were you as noble, as clever, as gentle, as wise, as good a provider, as rich in good deeds as Piedro could have been?"

~FROM "PIEDRO'S STORY", BY NOMI SHARRON

INTENTION: "I do what I can, with what I have, where I am."

or

Write your own: _____

_____

REFLECTIONS: Do you believe that you are doing the best you can, with what you have, where you are right now in your life? If you feel in your heart that perhaps you can't answer that in the affirmative, question your reasons, do some self-inquiry, and write about what you may do differently to change that.

Journey to the Self

13
PERFECT JUST THE
WAY YOU ARE

*"A WATER BEARER IN INDIA had two large pots, each
hanging on each end of a pole which he carried across
his neck. One of the pots had a crack in it, and while the other
pot was perfect and always delivered a full portion of water
at the end of the long walk from the stream to the master's
house, the cracked pot arrived only half full. For two years
this went on daily, with the bearer delivering only one and a
half pots of water to his master's house. Of course, the perfect
pot was proud of its accomplishments, perfect to the end for
which it was made. But the poor cracked pot was ashamed of
its imperfection and miserable that it was able to accomplish
only half of what it had been made to do. After two years of
what it perceived to be a bitter failure, it spoke to the water
bearer one day by the stream. 'I am ashamed of myself, and
I want to apologize to you.' 'Why?' asked the bearer. 'I have*

been able to deliver only half my load because the crack in my side causes water to leak out all the way back to your master's house. Because of my flaws, you have to do all of this work and you don't get full value from your efforts,' the pot said. The water bearer felt sorry for the old cracked pot and in his compassion he said, 'As we return to the master's house, I want you to notice the beautiful flowers along the path. Did you notice that there were flowers only on your side of the path, but not on the other pot's side? That's because I have always known about your flaw, and I took advantage of it. I planted flower seeds on your side of the path and every day while we walk back from the stream you've watered them. For two years I have been able to pick these beautiful flowers to decorate my master's table. Without you being just the way you are, he would not have this beauty to grace his house.'"

~"The Cracked Pot," a parable

INTENTION: "I accept myself as I am in this moment."

or

Write your own: _____

_____

"Love yourself, accept yourself, forgive yourself, and be good to yourself, because without you the rest of us are without a source of many wonderful things."

~Leo F. Buscaglia

REFLECTIONS: Rather than criticize yourself or another person for something you perceive as a weakness or flaw, see if knowing that "it is as it must be at this moment" changes your perception and experience. Journal about any areas in your life that you would like to change. Think of how you can make changes in your mindset to cultivate acceptance rather than resistance, and how that may better serve you.

_____

_____

_____

_____

_____

_____

_____

_____

_____

_____

_____

_____

_____

_____

14
CHOICES

EACH OF US HAS tremendous power over our own state of being.
So often we blame outside circumstances and other people for
our own happiness or misery, without realizing that our attitudes
and perceptions are within our own control. It's up to each of us to
acknowledge or relinquish control over our own lives. How often do
we hear people blame their childhoods or other past events for what
is happening today, maintaining a victim persona rather than one of
renewed strength? Think about it honestly: Do others *do* things to
you or do you *allow* them to do it? Do you look for and see only the
negative in a situation, or are you open enough to allow yourself to
see the positive?

"Be miserable. Or motivate yourself. Whatever has to be done, it's always your choice."

~Dr. Wayne Dyer

INTENTION: "I am responsible for my own happiness."

or

Write your own: _____

_____

"If you change the way you look at things, the things you look at change."

~Dr. Wayne Dyer

REFLECTIONS: Do you believe you are responsible for your own happiness? Reflect upon and list the people and circumstances that you blame for what you consider to be your present challenges or difficulties. Do some soul searching: Next to each item you listed, write about your role in the responsibility for your behavior. Journal about one step you can choose to do today toward your own happiness. Ask yourself what you can do tomorrow, then the next day, then the next, and the next....

\
\
\
\
\
\
\
\
\
\
\
\
\
\
\
\
\

15
THOUGHT VERSUS EXPERIENCE

A THOUGHT CAN BE A very dangerous weapon. "The smallest idea can define you or destroy you," it was said in the movie *Inception*. For example, the perceptions we have of ourselves often stem from thoughts, ideas and words from our childhoods and help to shape who we become. Negative words and ideas thrown at us as we're growing up may become the basis for our personae in the world. We often allow ourselves to believe these ideas rather than trust in our own experiences of ourselves. For example, perhaps you were told that you can't do anything right, and you assume that statement to be true rather than try to notice all of your accomplishments. Trust the voice of truth within your heart rather than the voice of the past within your head.

"The mind is everything.
What we think, we become."

~THE BUDDHA

INTENTION: "I trust the voice of truth within me."

or

Write your own: _____

_____

"Watch your thoughts, for they become words.
Watch your words, for they become actions.
Watch your actions, for they become habits.
Watch your habits, for they become character.
Watch your character, for it becomes destiny."

~AUTHOR UNKNOWN

REFLECTIONS: Leaving behind the judgment and critical voices from the past, journal about the positive qualities you possess that you are grateful for right at this moment in time.

_____

_____

_____

_____

_____

_____

_____

_____

_____

_____

_____

_____

_____

_____

_____

_____

_____

Journey to the Self

16
KEEP IT SIMPLE

BREATHING—just connecting to breath—can remind you of how simple it is to just "be." Notice where you are right now—how simple life is without judgments, without assigning labels of good and bad. Unfortunately, it seems to take a dramatic event or a tragedy to make one realize the beauty of simplicity, that the simplest joys are often quite enough to fill you with satisfaction and gratitude. People often lament not having the money or the time to go on a long trip to faraway places. However, perhaps truly being in the moment while sharing a good bottle of wine with a lover or friend, sitting in a beautiful garden, or taking an invigorating and inspiring hike, may be enough to feel that your heart is full and that it is enough.

"Enjoy the little things, for one day you may look back and realize they were the big things."

~ROBERT BRAULT

INTENTION: "I enjoy the positive in every experience."

or

Write your own: _____

_____

"Simplicity is about subtracting the obvious and adding the meaningful."

~JOHN MAEDA

REFLECTIONS: Bring your awareness to your breath as you go through your day. Without judgment, notice where you are and what you're doing: object, place, feeling, action and so on. Be mindful of what you're sitting or standing on, the touch of your clothes on your skin, the hair on your forehead, the sounds around you. Journal about the simple joys of your day.

_____

_____

_____

_____

_____

_____

_____

_____

_____

_____

_____

_____

_____

_____

_____

17
THE LIGHTNESS OF BEING

LETTING GO OF FEARS, regrets and worries is often difficult, even though we know they no longer serve us and in fact cause us pain and dis-ease. How refreshing it is to release those thoughts that haunt us and suddenly experience more air and deeper breaths, feeling lighter and walking taller! Once we stop trying to control the negative thoughts, comments, hurts and concerns that have weighed us down and depleted us emotionally for so long, we'll discover the freedom, empowerment and joy that results from just letting them go, like helium balloons flying up into the sky.

"Getting over a painful experience is much like crossing monkey bars. You have to let go at some point in order to move forward."

~AUTHOR UNKNOWN

INTENTION: "I release the thought that has been causing me pain."

or

Write your own: _____

_____

"People have a hard time letting go of their suffering. Out of a fear of the unknown, they prefer suffering that is familiar."

~THICH NHAT HANH

REFLECTIONS: List the thoughts, concerns and hurts that have been weighing you down and depleting your emotional reserves. Journal about what you might do to let each of them go; for example, connect the mind to breathe each time the thought intrudes or consciously turn to thoughts that make you happy. Perhaps create a personal ritual to let them go. Note what feelings and experiences result from this exercise in freedom.

_____

_____

_____

_____

_____

_____

_____

_____

_____

_____

_____

_____

_____

_____

_____

_____

_____

_____

_____

_____

_____

_____

_____

_____

_____

_____

_____

_____

_____

_____

_____

_____

_____

_____

_____

_____

18
LIGHTING THE PATH

SOMETIMES WE'RE IN NEED of a helping hand and a patient ear, and other times we're able to offer that to others. Sensitivity and awareness is often required to know where and how to receive what is needed or to offer it to others.

"We are not saints; we are not heroes. Our lives are lived in the quiet corners of the ordinary. We build tiny hearth fires, sometimes barely strong enough to give off warmth. But to the person lost in the darkness, our tiny flame may be the road to safety, the path to salvation. It is not given to us to know who is lost in the darkness that surrounds us or even if our light is seen...A sailor lost at sea can be guided home by a single candle. A person lost in a wood can be led to safety by a flickering flame. It is not an issue of quality or intensity or purity. It is simply an issue of the presence of light."

~KENT NERBURN

INTENTION: "I am a receiver and an instrument of light."

or

Write your own: _____

_____

"We cannot hold a torch to light another's path without brightening our own."

~BEN SWEETLAND

REFLECTIONS: Are you in need of light or help at this time and are you willing to request it? What gifts do you possess that might help you be the illumination for someone else in need?

_____

_____

_____

_____

_____

_____

_____

_____

_____

_____

_____

_____

_____

_____

_____

_____

Journey to the Self

19
PEACE OF MIND

I THINK THERE IS A mistaken belief that to be at peace with oneself necessitates the absence of all worries and human frailties; if this were the case, peace would never materialize! Life doesn't work this way for most people. It is in the awareness of all the various aspects that make up who we are that we can begin to tweak those things we choose to transform in a way that may better serve us. For instance, if we only come to the yoga mat when we can touch our toes or perfectly balance, we miss what yoga is truly about, being so much more than just the movement of the body. If we delay meditation for when the time is just right, we deprive ourselves of the beauty and benefits of sitting as quietly as we can and seeking physical, emotional and spiritual peace.

"Being at peace with ourselves is not about denying or rejecting any part of ourselves. On the contrary, in order to be at peace we must be willing and able to hold ourselves, in all our complexity, in a full embrace that excludes nothing. This is perhaps the most difficult part for many of us, because we want so much to disown the negative aspects of our humanity. Ironically, though, true peace begins with a willingness to take responsibility for our humanity so that we might ultimately transform it in the light of our love."

~MADISYN TAYLOR

INTENTION: "I accept and love myself as I am."

or

Write your own: _____

_____

"Sometimes life doesn't hand us what we want. And when we un-set our hearts from our needing it all to be a certain way, we can breathe a sigh of relief and open the door to a more powerful way of living."

~DR. SUSAN JEFFERS

REFLECTIONS: What arises in your mind while just sitting quietly? Sort out the destructive thoughts from the helpful ones, then think about how to let go of the former and act upon the latter.

_____

_____

_____

_____

_____

_____

_____

_____

_____

_____

_____

_____

_____

_____

_____

Journey to the Self

20
GENEROSITY

THINK ABOUT IT: Do you find yourself being more generous when you perceive yourself as having more and when you feel that your life is blessed? When you feel you have too little, do you still share your time or money? If you are expected to be generous with your time or your money, how do you react? Is your reaction dependent on the person or the circumstance, or don't these matter?

"The practice of generosity confronts us on several levels. It tests our trust in abundance. It tests our ability to empathize with others. And finally, it calls us on our sense of separation. The more 'different' we feel from other people, the harder it will be to give freely. The more we recognize that we are one and that other people's happiness is as important as ours, the more easily we can offer what we have. At the same time, acting generously strengthens our feeling of connectedness to the rest of the world. That's the true fruit of practicing generosity. Sooner or later, it will give us the insight that giving to others is really giving to ourselves—because in truth there is no other."

~YOGA JOURNAL NEWSLETTER, *WISDOM*

INTENTION: "I give to myself as well as to others."

or

Write your own: _____

_____

"Don't give until it hurts. Give until it feels good."

~RABBI MOSHE TUTNAUER

REFLECTIONS: Journal about the questions posed in this lesson on generosity. As a nightly exercise, answer the three "Naikan Practice" questions: What have you received today? What have you given today? What difficulties have you caused someone today?

_____

_____

_____

_____

_____

_____

_____

_____

_____

_____

_____

_____

_____

_____

Journey to the Self

21
RESISTANCE

D O YOU FEEL YOURSELF stuck in some area of your life, not able to move forward? Can you identify what it is that you are resisting—perhaps a change in attitude toward a person, situation or yourself? If you are practicing yoga asanas or any other physical activity, be aware of and locate that place in your body where you feel this resistance. Ask yourself what you may learn about yourself from this and listen carefully for the true answer. It may take a while, but once you hear the answer, ask yourself what would happen if you just let it go.

"Just as people want to be heard, so do our psychological states. Sometimes just listening to what your resistance wants to tell you is enough for it to open the gates and free you."

~SALLY KEMPTON

INTENTION: "I let _____ go and feel free."

or

Write your own: _____

_____

"The state of surrender is always a spontaneous rising, which you can allow to occur but never force. Someone I know describes his experiences of the state of surrender like this, 'I feel as if a bigger presence or energy pushes aside my limited agendas. When I feel it coming, I have a choice to allow it or resist it but it definitely comes from a place beyond what I think of as me and it always brings a huge sense of relief.'"

~SALLY KEMPTON

REFLECTIONS: When you identify the point of resistance within yourself in a situation, give yourself time to find its cause, ask what you can learn from it, see how you feel when you imagine letting it go…and then do it. Journal about the fear that might be holding you back from letting go. Once you locate the resistance and identify the fear, visualize what life would look like if you were to let it go. What is the worst that could happen if you let the resistance and fear go? If you can handle it, jump in with both feet. If not, keep working on it and try again when you feel more confident.

_____

_____

_____

_____

_____

_____

_____

_____

_____

_____

_____

_____

Journey to the Self

22

ONE STEP AT A TIME

You may walk through the days of your life without much thought, when suddenly a situation occurs that requires fortitude and definitive action—and you don't know where to start. Or, perhaps you discover a goal that you greatly desire but find to be daunting, and you have no idea where to begin. You're afraid to go forward and may even give up without trying. You may have heard it said that the way to eat an elephant is bite by bite. Indeed, taking things mindfully, step by step, keeps you present and enjoying each moment as you move forward along the way.

"If you go step by step, there will be no problems. Enjoy each step. Trying to leap many steps at once can be a problem."
~Sri T. Krishnamacharya

INTENTION: "I take things one step at a time."

or

Write your own: _____

_____

"One may walk over the highest mountain one step at a time."
~John Wanamaker

REFLECTIONS: List and journal about your goals and desires. For each goal write a step-by-step approach to attainment. Include a reasonable timetable, then start with one step at a time, enjoying each step along your way.

_____

_____

_____

_____

_____

_____

_____

_____

_____

_____

_____

_____

_____

_____

_____

_____

Journey to the Self

23
SWEET SURRENDER

"ISHVARA PRANIDHANA," OR "Surrender to the Divine," as explained by Patanjali in the Yoga Sutra 1:23, is not necessarily a theistic concept, nor is it the idea of giving up in the face of adversity. It can be taken as trusting in the order of the universe of which we are all a part. Just being alive inherently means the inevitability of illness, disappointments and difficulties, and there is great ease and peace of mind to be found in the acceptance of something beyond oneself whether from a religious, spiritual, or atheistic and scientific point of view. Trust that there is a plan to which you may not be privy and just go with the flow of it.

"Life may present you with any number of heartbreaks...Each of these instances is an opportunity to see that there can be great freedom and ease in letting go of the illusion of control over your circumstances."

~KATE HOLCOMBE

INTENTION: "I let go and trust in the natural flow of things."

or

Write your own: _____

_____

"You still hope, dream, or pray for and pursue what you want from life. But when things don't go as you had hoped, you trust that there is an order beyond your knowing or understanding. You can move forward with the peace that comes from accepting that the outcome is out of your hands, through surrender to something much bigger."

~KATE HOLCOMBE

REFLECTIONS: In moments of disappointment or difficulty, trust in and surrender to the divine order and find peace in knowing that all is as it should and must be in this moment. Just let go and see how that serves your inner quiet. Allow yourself a stream-of-consciousness flow of writing and journal about your reactions to letting go.

_____

_____

_____

_____

_____

_____

_____

_____

_____

_____

_____

_____

_____

_____

_____

_____

_____

_____

_____

_____

_____

_____

_____

_____

_____

_____

_____

_____

_____

_____

_____

_____

_____

Journey to the Self

24
NO PLACE LIKE OM

THERE MAY BE TIMES in your life when you feel that everything is falling apart around you, when you lose the very center of your being and feel very exposed and vulnerable. You may feel that the floor is dropping out from under you and question if you will ever feel alright again. These times of external shifts in your life are actually opportunities to analyze whether you have established your sense of identity and well-being in outward circumstances or within yourself. These more challenging times are a chance to rediscover and move closer to your core—that place of safety some call home and where your values and your strengths lie.

"Times of external darkness can be a great gift in that they provide an opportunity to remember this inner light that shines regardless of the circumstances of our lives. When our external lives begin to come back together, we are able to lean a bit more lightly on the structures we used to call home, knowing more clearly than ever that our true home is that bright sun shining in our core."

~MADISYN TAYLOR

INTENTION: "I trust and return to my core for strength."

or

Write your own: _____

_____

"People can't live with change if there's not a changeless core inside them. The key to the ability to change is a changeless sense of who you are, what you are about, and what you value."

~STEPHEN COVEY

REFLECTIONS: Try to access that sense of physical strength and stability in your physical core. Notice how this serves to enhance your emotional well-being and energy as well. Journal about your core values and whether or not you are able to keep them constant—whatever the circumstance.

_____

_____

_____

_____

_____

_____

_____

_____

_____

_____

_____

_____

_____

_____

Journey to the Self

25
BEING OKAY
WITH WHAT IS

BEING OKAY WITH what *is* does not mean that you enjoy hurt or frustration or that you should not try to improve painful situations. It is the recognition that in that moment, you cannot change that particular situation, so your choice is to be in the situation and fight each pain and frustration, or to be in the situation and redirect your thoughts to being okay then and there. Acceptance of what *is* does not mean passively shrugging your shoulders, giving up and feeling helpless. Rather, acceptance means facing the reality of "right now," knowing that it could be no different than how it is at that moment, while at the same time directing your positive energy toward the change that you want to happen. Feelings are not "right" or "wrong"; feelings don't have a story. It is the mind that assigns these labels. Therefore, you can choose to feed the mind by paying attention to it, or to refocus on feeling or breathing or some other way of pulling back, thereby finding objectivity in that moment and—hopefully—peace.

Stay in the moment of "what is," and within the ensuing calmness you can more mindfully respond rather than react to any situation.

"When we stop opposing reality, action becomes simple, fluid, kind, and fearless."

~BYRON KATIE

INTENTION: "I step outside of my experience and find peace."

or

Write your own: _____

_____

"Enlightenment is the quiet acceptance of what is. I believe the truly enlightened beings are those who refuse to allow themselves to be distressed over things that simply are the way they are."

~DR. WAYNE DYER

REFLECTIONS: Notice your reactions to various situations during the day. While in a stressful or frustrating situation, consciously bring your awareness to your breathing and see how that serves your peace and stillness. Journal about how you feel when you let go and deal with "what is" as opposed to what you feel "should be."

_____

_____

_____

_____

_____

_____

_____

_____

_____

_____

_____

_____

_____

_____

Journey to the Self

26

MAKING PEACE
WITH YOUR BODY

FOR HOW MANY YEARS have you been waging war on your body, fighting and resisting what and how it is, obsessing over how to finally "fix it"? How much pain has this been causing you? Whether the problem of poor self-image comes from a self-perception of being too heavy or too thin, having physical limitations due to injury, age or illness, having a history of abuse, or wanting your physical features to be different than they are, you may find that life is becoming an uphill battle of obsessive negative thoughts. Make peace with your body so you can move your attention from ego-centered self-judgment to what is really important in life. Connecting to breath and staying in the moment helps you to be aware of and appreciate those things your body *can* do, thereby indulging in less criticism and fault finding. Honor your body and yourself.

"Before we can find peace among nations, we have to find peace inside that small nation which is our own being."

~BKS. IYENGAR

INTENTION: "I am grateful that my body can _____."

or

Write your own: _____

_____

"In the beauty, wonder, and simplicity of the moment, there is less room for the endless projections of self-hatred, body-oriented criticism, and fear-based judgments."

~CHRISTINA SELL

REFLECTIONS: Soften, relax and listen to your body, treating it with compassion, appreciation and love. Rather than focus on your body's perceived deficiencies, list and journal about all that your body has done and can do for you.

_____

_____

_____

_____

_____

_____

_____

_____

_____

_____

_____

_____

_____

_____

_____

_____

Journey to the Self

27

THE RESTORATIVE POWER OF SILENCE

SILENCE. An occasion to look inward, to connect with the ambient sounds of nature, to increase awareness of ordinary moments. It is so easy to lose yourself in the busy-ness of your daily life, always postponing that time to reconnect and reacquaint with yourself until after this or that is done. It's easy to absorb the negative or frenetic energy from people or situations that may surround you, ignoring your inner warning to stay in an atmosphere of nourishment rather than toxicity. In these modern times, we are surrounded by noise, inside of our houses and out. It's easy to get lost within the noise and forget how much your health and spirit are enriched by the experience of silence. My experience has been that the more I bathe in silence, the more my "appetite for silence" grows.

"Silence has formed a foundation for me by providing the time and fertile space in which to reflect on the kind of life I want to have and the center from which to live it."

~ANNE LeCLAIRE

INTENTION: "I feel the presence of energy and beauty around me."

or

Write your own: _____

_____

"When we start meditating in silence, right from the beginning we feel the bottom of a sea within us and without. The life of activity, movement and restlessness is on the surface, but deep below, underneath our human life, there is poise and silence."

~SRI CHINMOY

REFLECTIONS: Think of simple ways you can experience the restorative power of silence during your day. Some examples might be spending some quiet time in nature, taking a break from e-mail, phone, and TV for even a day, sitting in meditation, or just closing your eyes and listening to the silence. Journal about your experiences and what you plan to continue to do in the days to come.

_____

_____

_____

_____

_____

_____

_____

_____

_____

_____

_____

_____

_____

_____

28
RANDOM ACTS
OF KINDNESS

WESTERN RELIGIONS and ethics promote the idea of "an eye for an eye" when dealing with adversaries. We also have the proverb, "Kill them with kindness," which is a bit closer to the Eastern ideal although the motivation is questionable. Eastern thought espouses that all things are connected and so actions must be considered as affecting more than just oneself. If we adhere to the philosophy of *Ahimsa,* or nonharming, we know that we must hold on to this ideal in relation to all people and all sentient beings. Our behavior must reflect our own values and beliefs in order for us to have stillness and peace of mind, no matter what others have done or said.

"Darkness cannot drive out darkness; only light can do that. Hate cannot drive out hate; only love can do that."

~DR. MARTIN LUTHER KING JR.

INTENTION: "I practice love for myself and others."

or

Write your own: _____

_____

"Focus, not on the rudeness of others, not on what they have done or left undone, but on what you have and haven't done yourself."

~DHAMMAPADA, 4

REFLECTIONS: Perform an act of kindness toward another person today, as well as toward yourself. Journal about how that makes you feel and what you can continue to do on subsequent days.

_____

_____

_____

_____

_____

_____

_____

_____

_____

_____

_____

_____

_____

_____

_____

Journey to the Self

29

FROM DARKNESS
TO LIGHT

YOGA CLASSES ARE OFTEN started with the *Asatoma* incantation, the Sanskrit chant that expresses the hope that our practice
will lead us

> ...from the unreal or the illusion *(maya)* of this life that we
> think is real, to the eternal truth.
>
> ...from darkness or ignorance *(avidya),* which Buddha said
> is "the mother of all problems," to the light of knowledge.
>
> ...from time-bound consciousness or sense of limitation to
> the timeless state of immortality, or spiritual awareness
> and limitless liberation.

Time-bound consciousness is such a large part of our lives, as
evidenced by our reliance upon our calendars to plan our days and
weeks, or our habit of flying from one appointment to the next. Imagine
just letting go and enjoying every moment, just as it is!

"Asatoma sadgamaya
Tamasoma jyotir gamaya
Mrityorma amritam gamaya"

~ASATOMA INCANTATION (IN SANSKRIT)

INTENTION: "I let go and enjoy each moment as it comes."

or

Write your own: _____

_____

"There is a fifth dimension, beyond that which is known to man. It is a dimension as vast as space and as timeless as infinity. It is the middle ground between light and shadow, between science and superstition."

~ROD SERLING

REFLECTIONS: How can you make more time in your schedule to make sure you can reflect upon and are present for each experience in your busy day?

_____

_____

_____

_____

_____

_____

_____

_____

_____

_____

_____

_____

_____

_____

_____

_____

Journey to the Self

30
GO WITH THE FLOW

THE BENEFIT OF PLIABILITY is often demonstrated in the analogy of a tree, which may break in a strong wind if inflexible and stiff, but can bend and sway in that wind when soft and allowing. Likewise, a person who is unbendable and rigid in his ways, beliefs and attitudes may more easily be broken by life's surprises and the very nature of the impermanence of life. If you can go with the flow of life and be open to whatever may come, you will weather the trials that come your way and perhaps even flourish. Staying open to whatever arises by not judging and labeling a situation as "good" or "bad" is one way to prepare yourself for being ready for anything that may occur in your day. If you aren't prepared to deal with the unpleasantries as well as the pleasantries, your rigidity may cause you to break during those times of adversity.

"A man is born gentle and weak; at his death he is hard and stiff.
All things, including the grass and trees, are soft and pliable in life;
dry and brittle in death.

Stiffness is thus a companion of death; flexibility a companion of life.
An army that cannot yield will be defeated.
A tree that cannot bend will crack in the wind.

The hard and stiff will be broken; the soft and supple will prevail."

~LAO TZU

INTENTION: "I breathe and sway with the flow of life."

or

Write your own: _____

_____

"Blessed are the flexible for they shall not be bent out of shape."

~MICHAEL MCGRIFFY, MD

REFLECTIONS: Notice your reaction when things don't go the way you had hoped or when the result is something unplanned. Are you able to be flexible and go with the flow, or are you rigid, without allowing for change?

_____

_____

_____

_____

_____

_____

_____

_____

_____

_____

_____

_____

_____

_____

Journey to the Self

31
NO ORDINARY MOMENTS

As you go through your day, it is easy to get caught up in the hectic pace of life and to put labels on what is significant and what is not. If you are open and fully present, you can experience and appreciate all those moments that are before you as precious—not just the ones that make you rich or famous, but rather the beauty that is everywhere in nature, a random act of pure kindness and love, the wonder of a baby's laughter, the life-saving epiphany of someone you care about. These moments are all around you if you take note of them and appreciate the joy that they add to your life. Indeed, there are no ordinary moments if you allow yourself to be touched by life.

"Walking, sitting, breathing, or taking out the trash deserve as much attention as a triple somersault."

~DAN MILLMAN

INTENTION: "I allow myself to be touched by the little things in life."

or

Write your own: _____

_____

"I've learned that the quality of each moment depends not on what we get from it, but on what we bring to it.…By treating every action with respect and every moment as sacred, I've found a new relationship with life, filled with passion and purpose."

~DAN MILLMAN

REFLECTIONS: It's all about awareness. Take the time to connect to breath, notice where you are, what is going on around you, and what you can bring to the moment. Journal about the little things you're noticing now that you may have missed before.

_____

_____

_____

_____

_____

_____

_____

_____

_____

_____

_____

_____

_____

_____

Journey to the Self

32
KIND WORDS

STICKS AND STONES may break your bones, but that's the only part of the childhood saying I agree with. Words can hurt deeply as well; they can break your spirit, your self-confidence and your heart. Just as you may have counted on and looked up to certain people in your life and have been or would be crushed if they were to verbally turn on you, realize that others look at you in this same way, others whom you can equally crush with cutting or critical remarks. Using Sai Baba's criteria of asking yourself whether what you want to say to someone is kind, true, necessary and will improve on the silence, can give you the time to pause and reflect before uttering something you might regret. Once unkind words leave your mouth, you can never erase the scars that may be left from them. Words have great power; wield them with care.

*"Better than a gift given with a joyous heart
are sweet words spoken with a cheerful smile."*

~THIRUKKURAL, 92

INTENTION: "I speak kindly to others and myself."

or

Write your own: _____

_____

*"Kindness is the language which the deaf can hear and the
blind can see."*

~MARK TWAIN

REFLECTIONS: Though we may be careful of what we say to others, it's curious that we often don't hesitate to criticize and belittle ourselves. Write a complimentary letter to yourself including all the positive and laudable things you have done and pat yourself on the back.

_____

_____

_____

_____

_____

_____

_____

_____

_____

_____

_____

_____

_____

_____

Journey to the Self

33
MAKING WISE CHOICES

YOU MAY FIND YOURSELF torn between several choices to which your ego mind is attached and, therefore, is telling you that you want. How do you know if what your heart or intuition tells you is good for you? One indication is your energy: Pay attention to what is uplifting or what is depleting you, including situations and people with whom you are in contact. How do you feel when you are with a person or in that particular situation? Another way of knowing is to tune in to your heart by going within through meditation or breath. Then there is that "gut feeling," a visceral, natural survival instinct, that along with the heart, taps into the body's intelligence and which, once again, you must learn to access and then trust.

"Thoughts are universally and not individually rooted; a truth cannot be created, but only perceived....The goal of yoga science is to calm the mind, that without distortion it may hear the infallible counsel of the Inner Voice."

~PARAMAHANSA YOGANANDA

INTENTION: "I trust my inner voice to know what is best for me."

or

Write your own: _____

_____

"May the long time sun shine upon you.
All love surround you.
And the light within you guide your way on."

~IRISH BALLAD

REFLECTIONS: You don't have to be on the mat or sitting in meditation in order to tune into a quiet place inside. With eyes open or closed, listen to what the heart is whispering, and "feel" what the gut is saying. Journal about how specific individuals and situations make you feel and why; perhaps they make you feel comfortable or uncomfortable, positive or depressed, high energy or drained of energy, and so on.

_____

_____

_____

_____

_____

_____

_____

_____

_____

_____

_____

_____

_____

_____

_____

Journey to the Self

34
LEARNING LESSONS

WE ALL KNOW PEOPLE who continue to make the same poor decisions time after time, then blame other people or the universe for their unhappiness. In yoga we learn the benefit of increased awareness and taking responsibility for our own actions. Knowing that our happiness is always within us and doesn't depend upon any outside source may give us the confidence and strength we need to take responsibility for our own decisions.

"I walk down the street. There's a deep hole in the sidewalk. I fall in. I am lost. I am hopeless. It isn't my fault. It takes me forever to find my way out.

I walk down the same street. There's a deep hole in the sidewalk. I pretend I don't see it. I fall in again. I can't believe I'm in the same place. It isn't my fault. It still takes me a long time to find my way out.

I walk down the same street. There's a deep hole in the sidewalk, I still fall in...it's a habit. My eyes are open, I know where I am. It is my fault. I get out immediately.

I walk down the same street. There's a deep hole in the sidewalk. I walk around it.

I walk down another street."

~SOGYAL RINPOCHE

INTENTION: "I take responsibility for my own decisions."

or

Write your own: _____

_____

"And the day came when the risk to remain tight in a bud was more painful than the risk it took to blossom."

~ANAIS NIN

REFLECTIONS: Journal about the habits that you would like to change and your answers to the following questions: Do you find yourself falling into the same hole time after time? Do you tend to blame others for your troubles or do you take responsibility for yourself? When you eventually realize that you may need to do things differently, are you able to find the strength to do that? What are your emotional responses when you are honest with yourself about your behavior?

_____

_____

_____

_____

_____

_____

_____

_____

_____

_____

_____

_____

35
EVERYTHING IS
LINKED TOGETHER

"YOGA" IN SANSKRIT means unity, union or joining. It is the unity of body, mind and spirit all working in concert; the unity of humankind, all one, made of the same life essence, sharing the same cosmic consciousness; the unity of all sentient beings, sharing the same air, space and time. Everything is linked, but until we can truly know this within our hearts, it remains ethereal. Yoga brings the stillness to the practitioner that is necessary for the seeing of that essential truth that yes, everything IS one.

"All life is interrelated. We are all caught in an inescapable network of mutuality, tied into a single garment of destiny.... We aren't going to have peace on earth until we recognize the basic fact of the interrelated structure of all reality."

~DR. MARTIN LUTHER KING JR.

INTENTION: "I am a part of everything around me."

or

Write your own: _____

_____

"Yoga exists in the world because everything is linked."

~T.K.V. DESIKACHAR

REFLECTIONS: Journal about the common threads you have with people and even animals you are in contact with throughout your day. Think in terms of needs, values and desires. How does that change your perspective and possibly your behavior, if at all?

_____

_____

_____

_____

_____

_____

_____

_____

_____

_____

_____

_____

_____

_____

_____

36
"Doing" Yoga

WE OFTEN HEAR PEOPLE say that they don't "do" yoga because they aren't very flexible or because they're out of shape. They look confused when I tell them that they "do" yoga each time they become aware of their own habits, connect to their breath in order to calm themselves in a situation, or perform an act of kindness for themselves or others. The physical mat practice is a place to learn about yourself: your habits, your patience level, your reaction to frustration, your ability to focus and find peace, and so many more things. It is within the poses that we learn to know ourselves, which is the essence of yoga itself.

"When we realize that what we are advancing toward is not some physical form, but an inward recognition of the truth of who we are, then we will not feel ourselves to be failing if we cannot attain difficult postures."

~DONNA FARHI

INTENTION: "I learn about myself from each situation."

or

Write your own: _____

_____

"Postures are concerned not really with any kind of physiological training, but an inner training of being—learning just to be."

~BHAGWAN SHREE RAJNEESH

REFLECTIONS: Notice your responses to the stimuli around you. Can you find the calm in the midst of the busy-ness and imperfections of your life? How do you see yourself in relation to your daily experience of your world? What other practices can you do to enhance peace in your life?

_____

_____

_____

_____

_____

_____

_____

_____

_____

_____

_____

_____

_____

_____

🪷 Journey to the Self

37

DOES MY EGO LOOK
FAT IN THESE JEANS?

WHEN WE'RE YOUNG we often spend so much time worry-ing about how we look that we ignore the spiritual side of our nature. There is great comfort and ease as we develop this spiritual component in our lives, at any age or stage, which gives us a greater ability to place the physical into a more realistic perspective. Of course, we want to keep our bodies healthy and comfortable, but the proper perspective is important for maintaining peace of mind.

"Remember how short this life is. Don't waste it. Understand that the shape of your body is irrelevant. The flexibility of your hamstrings or whether you can do a handstand is irrelevant. Those things are a distraction; they are vanity and ego. They have nothing to do with your highest potential—health and happiness through gentleness and awareness....Through this natural process [of yoga] life becomes rich regardless of the shape of your body or size of your bank account."

~BRYAN KEST

INTENTION: "I connect to breath and am grateful for being me."

or

Write your own: _____

_____

"It's also helpful to realize that this very body that we have, that's sitting right here right now...with its aches and its pleasures...is exactly what we need to be fully human, fully awake, fully alive."

~PEMA CHODRON

REFLECTIONS: Journal about all the positive attributes of your body just as it is right now. What do you count on it to do—day in, day out—that you can thank it for?

_____

_____

_____

_____

_____

_____

_____

_____

_____

_____

_____

_____

_____

_____

_____

_____

_____

Journey to the Self

38

NOURISHMENT
AND GROWTH

SPRING IS A TIME of beautiful, colorful flowers issuing forth after a winter of harsh weather. Just like germinating flower seeds, you need to nurture your body, mind and spirit, allowing your inner beauty to shine through. The seeds within you remain buried until outside conditions stimulate their growth, just as the rain and sunshine is needed for plants to thrive. Some of these seeds flourish on happiness and good things and bloom into beautiful flowers, while others, reacting to obstacles and pain, come forth as unsightly weeds. However, which seed will grow in reaction to which condition—either positive or negative—is unknown until a particular situation arises. In response you can choose to be trampled down completely, or to grow and thrive no matter what the emotional climate. Attitude and perspective color your days, and while the objective reality may not change, your response to it can, which is the only thing in your control after all.

"If there is a problem and there is nothing you can do about it, there is no use worrying.

If there is something that can be done, there is no use worrying.

And with that understanding can come contentment, even joy."

~THE DALAI LAMA

INTENTION: "I choose to nourish my body, mind and spirit."

or

Write your own: _____

_____

"Each morning when I open my eyes I say to myself: I, not events, have the power to make me happy or unhappy today. I can choose which it shall be. Yesterday is dead, tomorrow hasn't arrived yet. I have just one day, today, and I'm going to be happy in it."

~GROUCHO MARX

REFLECTIONS: Do you make the best of a situation by learning and growing from it, or do you allow the situation to trample you down, withered, into the soil? Mindfulness practices come into play here: breathing techniques, meditation, walks in nature, or any way that creates a place of quiet and peace within. Journal about the ways you find the quiet and peace you need to release from a stressful situation or tumultuous day.

_____

_____

_____

_____

_____

_____

_____

_____

_____

_____

_____

_____

_____

_____

39
DANGER OR
OPPORTUNITY?

LIFE INVOLVES CHANGE. You can get "stuck," longing for the way it used to be or the way you believe it's "supposed" to be, or you can "go with the flow" and allow a time of change to be a time for growth. Although the old familiar and comfortable ways may not work for you anymore, you see them as better options than taking a chance and trying something new. The Chinese character for crisis is a two-character word meaning both danger and opportunity. Which will you choose?

"Unless you try to do something beyond what you have already mastered, you will never grow."

~RALPH WALDO EMERSON

INTENTION: "I grab opportunity when it is presented to me."

or

Write your own: _____

_____

"As human beings, our greatness lies not so much in being able to remake the world—that is the myth of the atomic age—as in being able to remake ourselves."

~MOHANDAS GANDHI

REFLECTIONS: Your choice is to remain where you are or to grow by attempting change if you truly feel that would serve you best. List the opportunities presented to you that you might be hesitant or afraid to try. Then for each one write what you might gain if you would perceive it as an opportunity rather than a danger.

_____

_____

_____

_____

_____

_____

_____

_____

_____

_____

_____

_____

_____

_____

40
THE JUNK DRAWERS
OF OUR LIVES

THE CONCEPT OF PURITY *(Saucha)* in yoga is not just one of cleanliness, but also involves creating an atmosphere of nourishment in your life instead of toxicity. You are reminded to increase your awareness of how things in your daily experience serve you, including the food you eat, the music you hear, the entertainment you watch, or the people with whom you associate. You are encouraged to purge, remove and withdraw from the things that do not benefit you. Just as you can empty your junk drawer to make way for other possessions or just clean space, you can remove old self-perceptions and outdated views from your mind, making space for who you are today. It's about letting go—emotionally and physically.

"Sometimes you have to let everything go—purge yourself. If you are unhappy with anything—whatever is bringing you down—get rid of it. Because you will find that when you are free, your true creativity, your true self comes out."

~TINA TURNER

INTENTION: "I allow that which nourishes me into my life."

or

Write your own: _____

_____

"We must be willing to get rid of the life we've planned, so as to have the life that is waiting for us."

~JOSEPH CAMPBELL

REFLECTIONS: Be aware of the energy surrounding the food you eat, the entertainment you hear and see, and the people with whom you socialize. List those things in your life under "nourishing" or "toxic." What do you need to let go of and take in for greater peace and happiness?

_____

_____

_____

_____

_____

_____

_____

_____

_____

_____

_____

_____

_____

_____

_____

41
CREATING STILLNESS

How do you find stillness in the midst of your busy life, during a crisis, or when someone throws you an unexpected curve ball? Yoga's answer is to condition yourself to respond to these events by connecting to breath. Slowing down your breath and bringing your awareness to that breath will physiologically calm your nervous system, which in turn will quiet down your mind. Then you can respond to a situation mindfully, rather than panicking or reacting without forethought. Conditioning, however, comes with practice. Why not start right now?

"Only in quiet waters do things mirror themselves undistorted. Only in a quiet mind is adequate perception of the world."

~HANS MARGOLIUS

INTENTION: "I tap into the stillness within me."

or

Write your own: _____

_____

"In the midst of movement and chaos, keep stillness inside of you."

~DEEPAK CHOPRA

REFLECTIONS: Before reacting to a situation, take the time to connect to breath—even just a few deep breaths. Now respond to the situation and see if the breathing made a difference in your experience. Journal about how you may have reacted in the past without that mindful awareness.

_____

_____

_____

_____

_____

_____

_____

_____

_____

_____

_____

_____

_____

42
CULTIVATING PATIENCE

OUR SOCIETY ENCOURAGES immediate gratification of needs and desires, so much so that we become impatient and disappointed if we don't see the results of our actions right away. This holds true with starting a diet, learning a sport or an instrument, or beginning a yoga practice and waiting for flexibility or enlightenment. Instead, try taking it one day at a time, one pose at a time, one breath at a time. Then, reflect and reap the goodness of your effort.

"When you plant seeds in the garden, you don't dig them up every day to see if they have sprouted yet. You simply water them and clear away the weeds; you know that the seeds will grow in time. Similarly, just do your daily practice and cultivate a kind heart. Abandon impatience and instead be content creating the causes for goodness; the results will come when they're ready."

~BHIKSHUNI THUBTEN CHODRON

INTENTION: "I breathe in patience, I breathe out peace."

or

Write your own: _____

_____

"Patience in essence issues from a calm vital faith that all will unfold in its right sequence and due time."

~RAY POSNER

REFLECTIONS: Cultivate patience by first finding a place of quiet within yourself, which might be through meditation, mindful breathing, long walks in nature; find what works best for you. Then list some goals you would like to accomplish, choosing one to work on first. Write the series of steps you would need to take in order to accomplish this goal, and then go for it! How has the use of patience changed your experience?

_____

_____

_____

_____

_____

_____

_____

_____

_____

_____

_____

_____

_____

_____

_____

_____

_____

_____

_____

_____

_____

43
OPENING TO
NEW POSSIBILITIES

PERHAPS PEOPLE HAVE suggested that you take yoga, meditate, eat a healthier diet, or engage in behaviors they are sure will improve your life or help you find happiness or enlightenment. But perhaps you haven't heard them or have dismissed their suggestions as fluff or too "out there," firm in the belief that your way is best.

Then one day you take that class or feel a miraculous physical shift from some alternative healer. Perhaps you reap the rewards of a dietary cleanse or you take those deep breaths and discover the quiet inside. Suddenly, everyone is speaking your language; you're listening, not just accepting others to be "right" or "wrong," but opening your mind to the possibility of something else. You're displaying a willingness to try something new. Knowing that what you've been doing may not have been working for you, you're finally ready to listen and try something different.

"If you cling to an idea as the unalterable truth, then when the truth does come in person and knock at your door, you will not be able to open the door and accept it."

~UDANA SUTTA

INTENTION: "I am open to all possibilities."

or

Write your own: _____

_____

"When the student is ready, the master appears."

~BUDDHIST PROVERB

REFLECTIONS: Without jumping to conclusions or making judgments of right, wrong, good or bad, see if you can be open to really listening to others today. Journal about what people have said to you recently and how their words made you feel inside. Is it your usual habit to listen? Why or why not? What are your thoughts about this?

Journey to the Self

44
FEEL, DO, BE

ARE YOU SPENDING so much of your time searching for something you feel is missing that you don't take the time to enjoy what you *do* have? Of course it's necessary to know your direction and I'm certainly a proponent of mindfulness practices, but there comes a time when it's important to just let go and go with the flow of things, rather than over analyze everything. When you feel in your heart that the Way (Tao) is right, it's time to trust and let yourself be carried forward. You are a human BEing, not a human DOing, after all.

"The Sage has no need to affirm the Tao; he is far too busy enjoying it!"

~RAYMOND M. SMULLYAN

INTENTION: "I move into feeling and being."

or

Write your own: _____

_____

"The Tao has no purpose
and for this reason fulfills
all its purposes admirably."

~LAO TZU

REFLECTIONS: Treat yourself to something tasty today without counting calories or indulging in "shouldn'ts." Go to a movie or go shopping just because you want to! Journal about how you feel doing that, as well as your thoughts about those feelings.

_____

_____

_____

_____

_____

_____

_____

_____

_____

_____

_____

_____

_____

_____

_____

_____

Sandi Greenberg   175

45
READINESS

IF YOU'VE TRIED TO FORCE your body into a physical yoga pose or a gym exercise, or to participate in a sport before you were ready, you already know that you risk injury, pain and disappointment. You have to practice and warm up the muscles. Some movements may always be beyond your reach for whatever reason. Similarly, some goals and desires take a long time to achieve, even after a lot of warming up and preparation. You can't force certain things in life before you are ready for them, if ever. You can ease closer and closer to accomplishing your dreams, keeping an open mind so that you don't miss the opportunity when and if it presents itself. Then, wait for the way to be right, if it is indeed your path.

"If you spend too much time warming up, you'll miss the race. If you don't warm up at all, you may not finish the race."

~GRANT HEIDRICH

INTENTION: "I am willing to prepare for what I want in life."

or

Write your own: _____

_____

"You can't push anyone up the ladder unless he is ready to climb himself."

~ANDREW CARNEGIE

REFLECTIONS: Approach any personal disappointments with calm and compassion, knowing that your desires will be fulfilled if and when they are meant to be. Journal about times when you might have rushed into a situation before you were ready or when the time wasn't right. What were the results? Include times when the opposite may have been true.

_____

_____

_____

_____

_____

_____

_____

_____

_____

_____

_____

_____

_____

_____

_____

_____

Journey to the Self

46
SIMPLICITY

So OFTEN WE GET caught up in storytelling and over-dramatization of events, losing sight of reality. We begin to believe our exaggerated narrations and feel overwhelmed by what we've created for ourselves. This is the time to just stop, take some deep breaths, remember to take one step at a time, and gain a proper perspective of what is really going on. No more talking about it—just live it!

"Life is really simple, but we insist on making it complicated."

~CONFUCIUS

INTENTION: "I allow life to be simple and beautiful."

or

Write your own: _____

_____

"Any intelligent fool can make things bigger, more complex, and more violent. It takes a touch of genius—and a lot of courage—to move in the opposite direction."

~E.F. SCHUMACHER

REFLECTIONS: If an event upsets you, take a deep breath and notice if you are making the situation more complex than it needs to be. Let go and enjoy what is really going on without the added drama. List, then write about, the various problematic situations in your life and how you can make these situations simpler and their solutions less complicated.

_____

_____

_____

_____

_____

_____

_____

_____

_____

_____

_____

_____

_____

_____

Journey to the Self

47
THE RIGHT TIME
IS RIGHT NOW

B USY, BUSY; there's no time for yoga, meditation, or any spiritual practice, you say. You'll do it later. But isn't daily life, with its ups and downs, errands and obligations, changes and challenges, delights and disappointments, the very substance of a strong practice? You're in the middle of it all, every day, in some way. Your life is your practice. When all goes smoothly, you may not feel the need to look deeper within and develop yourself or to work hard toward greater growth. Rather, it is in your unhappiest moments—most unsatisfied or least comfortable—that the motivation arises to step out of the rut and seek a different path to finding the important answers to life.

*"Life's challenges are not supposed to paralyze you,
they're supposed to help you discover who you are."*

~Bernice Johnson Reagon

Intention: "My life is my practice."

or

Write your own: _____

_____

*"Look at a day when you are supremely satisfied at the end.
It's not a day when you lounge around doing nothing; it's when
you've had everything to do, and you've done it."*

~Margaret Thatcher

REFLECTIONS: As you meet various challenges during your day, note what you can learn from them. Give yourself time for some reflection. Journal about lessons learned, if any, and what your next steps will be for further growth.

_____

_____

_____

_____

_____

_____

_____

_____

_____

_____

_____

_____

_____

_____

_____

_____

Journey to the Self

48
LESS IS MORE

NO DOUBT YOU'VE SEEN television programs about people fleeing their homes during a natural disaster. What do they grab to take with them? What would you take in the same situation? Look around your home and ask yourself how much of what you own is really necessary for your happiness. Are you so attached to your material possessions that you'd be crushed if you lost them? People tend to lose sight of spiritual priorities in this materialistic world, where more is more and most is best. Sometimes a little jolt of reality or a change of scenery is needed to put things into a different perspective.

"I like to go camping. With limited space, you see how little a person really needs to be happy. Cooking over a gas stove forces you to slow down, cook and eat slowly, and pay attention to your surroundings."

~Shraga Hecht

Intention: "I let go of _____ to make space for _____".

or

Write your own: _____

_____

"Wake up! If you knew for certain you had a terminal illness—if you had little time left to live—you would waste precious little of it! Well, I'm telling you, you do have a terminal illness: It's called birth. You don't have more than a few years left. No one does! So be happy now, without reason—or you will never be at all."

~Dan Millman

REFLECTIONS: List some of the troublesome thoughts, people, places, and things you could let go of that would simplify and de-clutter your life. Journal about the results of that purging and how you feel.

_____

_____

_____

_____

_____

_____

_____

_____

_____

_____

_____

_____

_____

_____

_____

_____

_____

49
LAUGHTER IS THE
BEST MEDICINE

L AUGHTER IS AN IMPORTANT factor in our health, healing,
levels of stress and balancing of emotions. It is a powerful tool in
fighting many mental and physical illnesses; laughter also makes each
experience so much more fun. Everyone has the choice to respond
to adversity with negativity and fear or to respond with love and
positivity, making the best out of any situation. Even a forced smile
or laugh initiates an internal de-stressing and softening, which could
lead to a genuine smile. Do you remember participating in a laughter
chain when you were young, with each person lying on the belly of
another? The first person's belly laugh was all it took for everyone to
let go and roar! What a healthy and easy remedy!

"Laughter increases circulation, stimulates the immune system, exercises the muscles, and even invigorates the brain. Laughter reduces stress hormones and may even help prevent heart disease."

~WILLIAM FRY, MD

INTENTION: "I smile and laugh whenever possible."

or

Write your own: _____

_____

"What soap is to the body, laughter is to the soul."

~YIDDISH PROVERB

REFLECTIONS: Smile as you go through your day, both at others and to yourself. If occasions arise where laughter bubbles up within you, let it go out into the world. We need more of it! Journal about the effect your smile or laughter has on others around you and on your own experience. If you don't laugh often, write about why you think that might be and what you might do to remedy your lack of laughter.

_____

_____

_____

_____

_____

_____

_____

_____

_____

_____

_____

_____

_____

_____

_____

Journey to the Self

50
LIFE IS YOUR GURU

*G*URU IN SANSKRIT means "one who turns darkness into light." People often long to find such a spiritual teacher or guide and spend years seeking just the right person. The search often leads to frustration at the time spent, and can also lead to disappointment with the realization that the guru is indeed human and thus subject to human flaws. Yet, the greatest teacher you could ever want is always with you: it is your own life. When you are open to receiving and learning, the people and situations you encounter every day have much wisdom to teach you. Some show you what you want to do and be, and some teach by showing what you don't want to do or be.

"All the situations in our lives, from the insignificant to the major, conspire to teach us exactly what we need to be learning at any given time. Patience, compassion, perseverance, honesty, letting go—all these are covered in the classroom of the teacher that is your life. A difficult phase in your relationship with your child may be teaching you to let go. The homeless person you see every day may be showing you the boundaries of your compassion and generosity. A spate of lost items may be asking you to be more present to physical reality. Trust your intuition on the nature of the lesson at hand, work at your own pace, and ask as many questions as you want. Your life has all the answers."

~MADISYN TAYLOR

INTENTION: "I acknowledge and honor my life as a teacher."

or

Write your own: _____

_____

"In every moment of your life, you can use the events that occur and the people you interact with as signposts, mirrors and guides to your own particular issues that need work."

~LAURA BRYANNAN

REFLECTIONS: Take some time to consider what your life is trying to teach you through the various experiences in your day. Do the lessons ring true with your inner sense of knowing and can you act upon them mindfully? Journal about each experience and the lesson you feel is inherent within it.

_____

_____

_____

_____

_____

_____

_____

_____

_____

_____

_____

_____

_____

51
CHOOSE TO LIVE A LIFE
THAT MATTERS

"*READY OR NOT, some day it will all come to an end.
There will be no more sunrises, no minutes, hours or
days. All the things you collected, whether treasured or forgot-
ten, will pass to someone else. Your wealth, fame and temporal
power will shrivel to irrelevance. It will not matter what you
owned or what you were owed. Your grudges, resentments,
frustrations, and jealousies will finally disappear.*

*So, too, your hopes, ambitions, plans, and to-do lists will
expire. The wins and losses that once seemed so important
will fade away. It won't matter where you came from, or on
what side of the tracks you lived, at the end. It won't matter
whether you were beautiful or brilliant. Even your gender and
skin color will be irrelevant.*

*So what will matter? How will the value of your days be
measured? What will matter is not what you bought, but what*

you built; not what you got, but what you gave. What will matter is not your success, but your significance. What will matter is not what you learned, but what you taught. What will matter is every act of integrity, compassion, courage or sacrifice that enriched, empowered or encouraged others to emulate your example.

What will matter is not your competence, but your character. What will matter is not how many people you knew, but how many will feel a lasting loss when you're gone. What will matter are not your memories, but the memories that live in those who loved you. What will matter is how long you will be remembered, by whom and for what. Living a life that matters doesn't happen by accident. It's not a matter of circumstance, but of choice. Choose to live a life that matters."

~ANONYMOUS

INTENTION: "I choose to live a life that matters."

or

Write your own: _____

_____

"You are creating your legacy every minute of every day."

~SANDI GREENBERG

REFLECTIONS: How will you live a life that matters? What have you built or have you given? What memories will you leave behind? What can you contribute to your world in your own way that you would be proud to leave as your legacy? Are you creating your legacy by your behavior in your interactions with the people you love? Journal about your contributions to the world and what you might do differently.

_____

_____

_____

_____

_____

_____

_____

_____

_____

_____

_____

_____

_____

_____

_____

_____

_____

52
THE JOURNEY
CONTINUES

THE JOURNEY TO THE Self continues throughout your lifetime, with life lessons always presenting themselves to those who practice mindful awareness and who possess an open mind. You can learn from any obstacles in your path, from the people and animals in your life, from the myriad situations in your day.

"We have stories to tell, stories that provide wisdom about the journey of life. What more have we to give one another than our 'truth' about our human adventure as honestly and as openly as we know how?"

~RABBI SAUL RUBIN

INTENTION: "I am open to learning life's lessons."

or

Write your own: _____

_____

"Some stories don't have a clear beginning, middle and end. Life is about not knowing, having to change, taking the moment and making the best of it, without knowing what's going to happen next. Delicious ambiguity."

~GILDA RADNER

REFLECTIONS: During or at the close of each day, review the lessons you may have learned about yourself or your world. Journal about these lessons and how they may change your behavior or your attitudes in the future. Are you ready to continue life's amazing journey to your Self?

_____

_____

_____

_____

_____

_____

_____

_____

_____

_____

_____

_____

_____

_____

Journey to the Self

MANY THANKS...

MY ENDURING GRATITUDE goes to my wonderful family, without whom this book, and my personal journey, would not have been possible. My amazing husband Mark has once again been a daily source of encouragement and support, patiently giving me his time and his feedback as I bounce ideas and emotions off of him. My love and appreciation go to my children, Shira, Eytan and Joy, and Lindsey for their interest and inspiration throughout the creation of this book, and for just being the beautiful people that they are.

I thank my friends and relatives who have encouraged me on my way, and I bow to my many teachers and students from whom I have received so much wisdom, love, and light.

I am grateful to my daughter, Shira, and dear friend, Helene Sabel, for graciously sharing their valuable time in editing and commenting on the various revisions of this manuscript. And hats off to the creative team at 1106 Design for their professionalism, talent, support, and good nature throughout this project.

My humble thanks to you all. Namasté.

NOTES

INTRODUCTION

- Phillip Moffitt, "Self-discovery," in *Yoga Journal*, June, 2012

LESSON

1: Living and Loving the Journey
   - A.A. Milne (1882–1956), *The House on Pooh Corner*, 1966 edition, pg. 130
   - Author Unknown

2: Feeling Alive
   - Kahlil Gibran (1883–1931), *The Forerunner: His Parables and Poems*, 2000 edition
   - Mark Twain (1835–1910), American author and humorist

3: Perspective
   - The Dalai Lama, the 14th Dalai Lama, his holiness Tenzin Gyatso (1935)
   - Krishna Das (1947), American vocalist of *kirtan*, Indian devotional music

4: How Is That Working for You?
  - Tony Robbins (1960), American self-help author and motivational speaker
  - Albert Einstein (1879–1955), German physicist who is often regarded as the father of modern physics

5: Attachment to Results
  - Mel Campbell, "Going with the Flow", Sept. 1, 2011, *yogawithmel.wordpess.com*
  - Ralph Waldo Emerson (1803–1882), American essayist, lecturer and poet

6: Freedom
  - Antoine de Saint-Exupery (1900–1944), French writer and aviator
  - Walt Whitman (1819–1882), from "Song of the Open Road", lines 1–5, American poet, essayist and journalist

7: Dealing with Reality
  - Eckhart Tolle (1948), from *Oneness with All Life*, 2008, German-born Canadian writer
  - Stephen Cope, from *The Wisdom of Yoga*, psychotherapist, author and senior Kripalu Yoga teacher

8: Appreciation
  - Brooke "Medicine Eagle" Edwards, author and workshop presenter
  - The Dalai Lama

9: All About Attitude
  - The Eagles, from the song "Already Gone", in the 1974 album "On the Border"
  - Author Unknown

10: Validation
  – Nelson Mandela (1918), in "Invictus" (movie), South African politician, civil rights activist, and past president of South Africa 1994–1999
  – Leo Buscaglia (1924–1998), American author and motivational speaker

11: All things in Moderation
  – Julia Child (1912–2004), American chef, author, and television personality
  – Carl Gustave Jung (1875–1961), Swiss psychiatrist, psychologist and author

12: The Best You Can Be
  – Nomi Sharron, Israeli actress and author of *Tony Samara: A Modern Shaman…and Beyond* (2010)

13: Perfect Just the Way You are
  – "The Cracked Pot," a parable
  – Pema Chodron (1936), American-born Buddhist monk, author and teacher

14: Choices
  – Dr. Wayne Dyer (1940), American self-help author and lecturer
  – Dr. Wayne Dyer

15: Thought Versus Experience
  – The Buddha (c.563–483 BCE), Siddharta Gautama, Indian spiritual teacher, considered to be the first "awakened being" in most Buddhist traditions
  – Author Unknown

16: Keep it Simple
   – Robert Brault, freelance writer
   – John Maeda (1966–), graphic designer, computer scientist, and author

17: The Lightness of Being
   – Author Unknown
   – Thich Nhat Hanh (1926), Vietnamese Buddhist monk, teacher, author, poet, and peace activist who now lives in France

18: Lighting the Path
   – Kent Nerburn, from *Make Me an Instrument of Your Peace*, American author, sculptor, and educator
   – Ben Sweetland, American author

19: Peace of Mind
   – Madisyn Taylor, in *Daily Om*, November 14, 2010
   – Dr. Susan Jeffers, American author, life coach and speaker

20: Generosity
   – "Wisdom," *Yoga Journal Newsletter*, November 22, 2010
   – Rabbi Moshe Tutnauer (1934–2010), American-born rabbi and international speaker

21: Resistance
   – Sally Kempton, author and spiritual teacher
   – Sally Kempton

22: One Step at a Time
   – Sri T. Krishnamacharya (1888–1989), Indian yoga teacher, ayurvedic healer and scholar
   – John Wanamaker (1838–1922), American merchant, politician and religious leader

23: Sweet Surrender
  - Kate Holcombe, "The Sun Always Rises," *Yoga Journal*, December, 2010, yoga teacher and writer
  - Kate Holcombe, "The Sun Always Rises," *Yoga Journal*, December, 2010

24: No Place Like Om
  - Madisyn Taylor, in *Daily Om*, January 31, 2012
  - Stephen Covey, (1932), from *The Seven Habits of Highly Effective People*

25: Being Okay with What Is
  - Byron Katie (1942), American motivational speaker and author
  - Dr. Wayne Dyer

26: Making Peace with Your Body
  - B.K.S. Iyengar (1918), Indian-born founder of Iyengar Yoga, author and teacher
  - Christine Sell, psychologist and psychotherapist

27: The Restorative Power of Silence
  - Anne LeClaire, "The Quiet Revolution," *Yoga Journal*, June, 2009
  - Sri Chinmoy, (1931–2007), Indian spiritual teacher and philosopher

28: Random Acts of Kindness
  - Dr. Martin Luther King Jr. (1929–1968), American clergyman and civil-rights activist
  - Dhammapada, 4, a Buddhist scripture traditionally ascribed to the Buddha himself, translation by Thanissaro Bhikkhu

29: From Darkness to Light
  - Asatoma Incantation
  - Rod Serling, "The Twilight Zone", American TV series (1959–1964)

30: Go with the Flow
  - Lao Tzu, *Tao Te Ching*, #76 (often also written Tsu, Tse, Tze)
  - Michael McGriffy, MD

31: No Ordinary Moments
  - Dan Millman, *No Ordinary Moments*, pg. xvi, 1991
  - Dan Millman, *No Ordinary Moments*, pg. xvi, 1991

32: Kind Words
  - Tirukkural, 92, a Tamil text, authored between 2nd century BCE—5th century CE
  - Mark Twain

33: Making Wise Choices
  - Paramahansa Yogananda, *Autobiography of a Yogi*, pg. 178
  - Irish Ballad

34: Learning Lessons
  - Sogyal Rinpoche (1947), Tibetan Buddhist lama and teacher, and author of *The Tibetan Book of Living and Dying*
  - Anais Nin (1903–1977), French-Cuban author

35: Everything Is Linked Together
  - Dr. Martin Luther King Jr.
  - T.K.V. Desikachar (1938), son and student of Sri Krishnamacharya, Indian author, yoga teacher and scholar

36: "Doing" Yoga
- Donna Farhi, *Bringing Yoga to Life: The Everyday Practice of Enlightened Living*, 2003
- Bhagwan Shree Rajneesh, *Yoga: Science of the Soul*, pg. 16, 1984

37: Does My Ego Look Fat in These Jeans?
- Bryan Kest, http://www.poweryoga.com/aboutyoga/article.php
- Pema Chodron

38: Nourishment and Growth
- The Dalai Lama
- Groucho Marx (1890–1977), American comedian, film and TV star

39: Danger or Opportunity?
- Ralph Waldo Emerson
- Mohandas Gandhi (1869–1948), leader of Indian nationalism, led India to independence, inspired non-violence and civil-rights worldwide

40: The Junk Drawers of Our Lives
- Tina Turner (1939–), American singer and writer
- Joseph Campbell (1904–1987), American mythologist, writer and lecturer

41: Creating Stillness
- Hans Margolius (1902), German philosopher
- Deepak Chopra (1946), Indian-born American physician, motivational speaker, and author of self-help and spiritual books.

42: Cultivating Patience
- Bhikshuni Thubten Chodron (1950), American Tibetan Buddhist, best known for cultivating interfaith dialogue, creating Dharma outreach programs in prisons, and teaching her beliefs.
- Ray Posner

43: Opening to New Possibilities
- Udana Sutta, a Buddhist scripture, often translated as "inspired utterances"
- Buddhist Proverb

44: Feel, Do, Be
- Raymond M. Smullyan (1919), American author, Taoist philosopher, mathematician, logician, and magician, from *The Tao is Silent*, 1977
- Lao Tzu

45: Readiness
- Grant Heidrich
- Andrew Carnegie (1835–1919), Scottish-American industrialist and philanthropist

46: Simplicity
- Confucius
- E.F. Schumacher (1911–1977), German-born economist

47: The Right Time Is Right Now
- Bernice Johnson Reagon (1942), singer, composer, scholar and social activist
- Margaret Thatcher (1925), Former and longest-serving British prime minister, 1979–1990

48: Less Is More
- Shraga Hecht, Israeli tour guide
- Dan Millman, *The Way of the Peaceful Warrior*, 2000, pg. 185

49: Laughter Is the Best Medicine
- William Fry, MD
- Yiddish Proverb

50: Life Is Your Guru
- Madisyn Taylor, "Your Perfect Teacher," *Daily Om*, October 28, 2011
- Laura Bryannan

51: Choose to Live a Life That Matters
- Anonymous
- Sandi Greenberg

52: The Journey Continues
- Rabbi Saul Rubin, rabbi at Temple Beth Tefillot in Brunswick, Georgia since 1986
- Gilda Radner (1946–1989), American comedian and actress

CPSIA information can be obtained at www.ICGtesting.com
Printed in the USA
BVOW03s0329161213

338568BV00010B/15/P